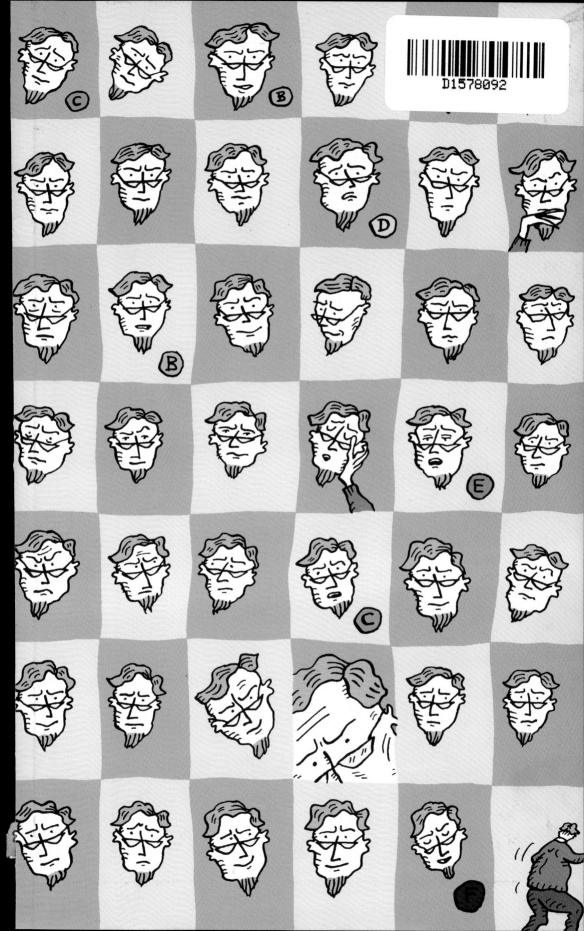

Mr Concerned's TALKING BOOK of HOME THERAPY

Next!

By STEVEN APPLEBY

Mr Segue Concerned, B.A.T., B.O.F.F., B.I.F.F., B.U.T.T.

Accredited by S.I.T. Discredited by W.H.T.R.O.T.
Approved by N.O.T.W.O.O.T. Disapproved by F.I.N.

Segue 'Jim' Concerned studied under many of the world's most eminent psychotherapists and counsellors before becoming the most eminent of them all.

He is the author of over seventy-nine books and has appeared on countless radio and television programmes.

He divides his time between his two children, Cornwallis and Saskatchewan, and his twelve homes.

WELCOME!

Dear client,

You hold in your hands a complete therapeutic manual. A mechanic for the mind. A course of therapy that would, in conventional hourly sessions, take many years and a great deal of money to complete.

Instead, you'll achieve the same results in a fraction of the time, at a fraction of the cost and without medication!

Whether you have a few nuts, bolts and screws loose, or merely want to do a little self-exploration in the hope of finding yourself, this book is YOUR answer!

Now, read on...

Your new best friend,

Segue 'Tim' Concerned

B.A.T., B.O.F.F., B.I.F.F., B.U.T.T.

For my Mum & Dad, who didn't
f**k me up Too badly... Or did they?!
Oh God, I don't know!

Many thanks to:
Jon Barraclough; Nick Battey; Pete Bishop (who inspired
all this by inventing the positive affirmation doll on page 60);
Jonny Boatfield; Penny Bradshaw; Karen Brown; Liz Calder;
Mary Clare Foa; Kasper de Graaf; David Jones; Janny Kent;
Linda McCarthy; Polly Napper; Sally Openshaw (special
adviser); Kerry Shale; Nicola Sherring; Mary Tomlinson;
Alan Wherry; and, of course, EVERYONE at Bloomsbury —
the best publisher in the world!

Voice of Mr Concerned: Kerry Shale
Recorded at: Q Two studios, London

First published 2002
Copyright Steven Appleby 2002
The moral right of the author has been asserted
Bloomsbury Publishing PLC, 38 Soho Square, London W1D 3HB

Reproduction by SC (Sang Choy) International Pte Ltd, Singapore
Printed & bound by C&C Offset Printing Co., Ltd., Hong Kong

ISBN: 0 7475 6073 0

SOME OF THE CONTENTS

PART 1

WHAT WENT WRONG?

THE RAW MATERIAL

OR

CLEAN SLATE*

*Clean, that is, except for the inherited characteristics.

TO FIND OUT HOW <u>YOU</u>, DEAR CLIENT, BECAME THE MESSED-UP PERSON YOU ARE TODAY, LET'S BEGIN BY LOOKING AT THE INNER WORKINGS OF THIS SMALL CHILD'S MIND...

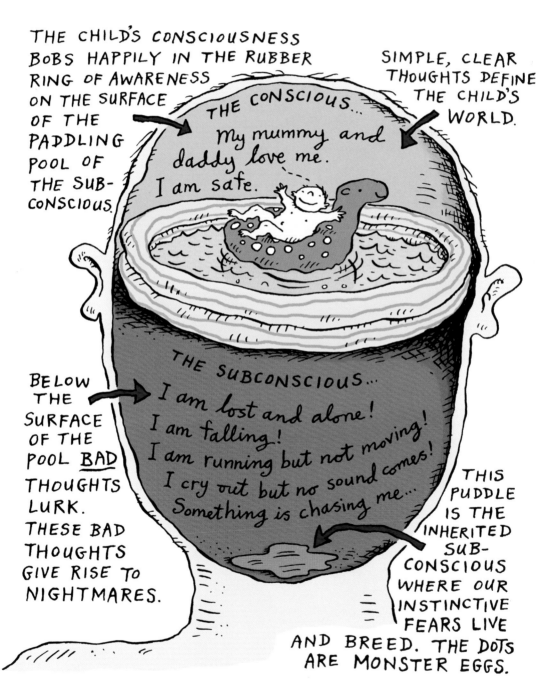

THE CHILD'S CONSCIOUSNESS BOBS HAPPILY IN THE RUBBER RING OF AWARENESS ON THE SURFACE OF THE PADDLING POOL OF THE SUB-CONSCIOUS.

SIMPLE, CLEAR THOUGHTS DEFINE THE CHILD'S WORLD.

THE CONSCIOUS...
My mummy and daddy love me. I am safe.

BELOW THE SURFACE OF THE POOL <u>BAD</u> THOUGHTS LURK. THESE BAD THOUGHTS GIVE RISE TO NIGHTMARES.

THE SUBCONSCIOUS...
I am lost and alone!
I am falling!
I am running but not moving!
I cry out but no sound comes!
Something is chasing me...

THIS PUDDLE IS THE INHERITED SUB-CONSCIOUS WHERE OUR INSTINCTIVE FEARS LIVE AND BREED. THE DOTS ARE MONSTER EGGS.

AS THE CHILD GROWS UP HE ABSORBS THE VIEWS AND OPINIONS OF THE PEOPLE AROUND HIM.

MUM AND DAD: He's a disappointment. We were hoping for a girl.

UNCLE GAS: He lets his pets die. He hasn't got an ounce of common sense.

PET: I never liked him.

SCHOOL-TEACHER: He means well but he's a day-dreamer...

BIG SISTER: He's DUMB!

LITTLE BROTHER: He's DUMB!

I am Buzz Lightyear! A hero!

UNCLE FERNANDO: He likes pink. I expect he's gay.

OTHER KIDS AT SCHOOL: He's no good at sport. He's soppy!

FIRST BOSS: Hmm... No drive. No ambition. I don't trust him.

TELEVISION: The world is out to get you! It's full of bad people.

FIRST GIRLFRIEND: He's got small private parts.

ADVERTISEMENTS: THIS IS WHAT REAL MEN LOOK LIKE! You wimp!

AND IN CONCLUSION: I am not Buzz Lightyear. I am a useless human being.

10

LET'S LOOK AGAIN AT THE SAME MIND A FEW YEARS LATER:

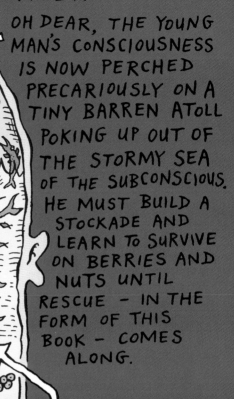

OH DEAR, THE YOUNG MAN'S CONSCIOUSNESS IS NOW PERCHED PRECARIOUSLY ON A TINY BARREN ATOLL POKING UP OUT OF THE STORMY SEA OF THE SUBCONSCIOUS. HE MUST BUILD A STOCKADE AND LEARN TO SURVIVE ON BERRIES AND NUTS UNTIL RESCUE — IN THE FORM OF THIS BOOK — COMES ALONG.

THE SUBCONSCIOUS HAS SWOLLEN INTO A VAST OCEAN STUFFED FULL OF THE NAKED, SLIMY MONSTERS OF CHILDHOOD. THESE MONSTERS, GROWN HUGE AND BREEDING FIERCELY, MUST BE FOUGHT AND DEFEATED OR THEY WILL SABOTAGE ALL ATTEMPTS THE CONSCIOUS MAKES TO ACHIEVE CONTENTMENT.

THE INHERITED SUBCONSCIOUS HAS GROWN FROM A SHALLOW PUDDLE INTO A SEETHING VOLCANIC HELL OF PRIMORDIAL INSTINCTIVE FEARS SUCH AS MUM'S TERROR OF SNAKES AND DAD'S FEAR OF DEEP, DARK HOLES WITH TEETH IN THEM!

HOW HAS SUCH A CHANGE COME ABOUT? THE ANSWER LIES IN THE WORKINGS OF THE BRAIN...

1 — THE SELF-IMAGE FILTER SORTS INCOMING INFORMATION. POSITIVE COMMENTS ARE DISMISSED AND TOSSED INTO THE WASTE-BASKET OF FAR-FETCHED THOUGHTS.

NEGATIVE COMMENTS ARE POUNCED UPON, AMPLIFIED AND CARVED ONTO TINY STONE TABLETS WHICH CIRCULATE FOREVER.

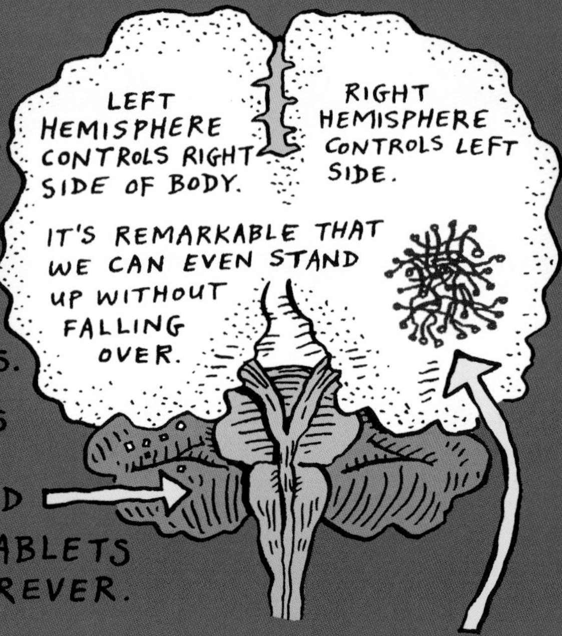

LEFT HEMISPHERE CONTROLS RIGHT SIDE OF BODY.

RIGHT HEMISPHERE - CONTROLS LEFT SIDE.

IT'S REMARKABLE THAT WE CAN EVEN STAND UP WITHOUT FALLING OVER.

2 — EACH NEW PIECE OF INFORMATION CAUSES STRING-LIKE PATHS TO OPEN UP BETWEEN BRAIN CELLS. AS INFORMATION FLOODS IN THROUGHOUT CHILDHOOD AND THESE PATHS MULTIPLY, THEY ARE SOON THOROUGHLY TANGLED AND MIXED-UP.

THIS DIAGRAM SHOWS THE FUNCTIONS OF VARIOUS SPECIFIC AREAS OF THE BRAIN:

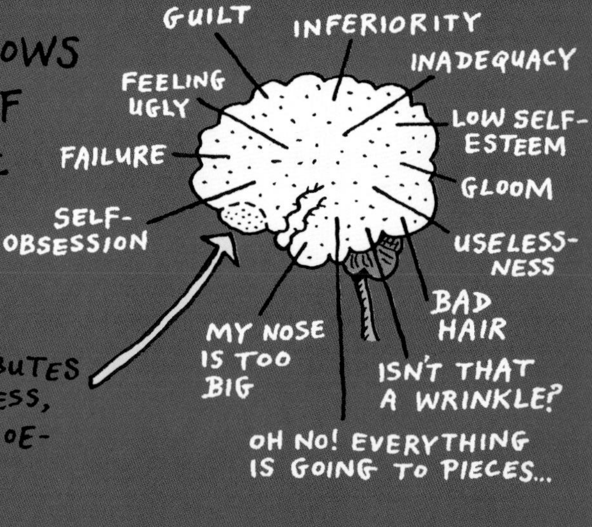

GUILT
INFERIORITY
INADEQUACY
FEELING UGLY
LOW SELF-ESTEEM
FAILURE
GLOOM
SELF-OBSESSION
USELESS-NESS
BAD HAIR
MY NOSE IS TOO BIG
ISN'T THAT A WRINKLE?
OH NO! EVERYTHING IS GOING TO PIECES...

ALL OPTIMISTIC ATTRIBUTES (SUCH AS HOPE, HAPPINESS, KINDNESS, ETC.) ARE SHOE-HORNED INTO A SMALL REGION DOWN HERE.

HERE IS AN EXAMPLE OF HOW THE BRAIN COLLECTS, COLLATES AND DRAWS CONCLUSIONS FROM INFORMATION:

1. Mummy and Daddy love me. I am safe.

2. SHORTLY... Now they have left me in a cot... ALONE! Mummy and Daddy DO NOT love me!! WAAAA!!

3. SOON. Mummy has come back and she is feeding me. Is this because she loves me after all, or was I right the first time? If I was right and she doesn't love me, then perhaps she is fattening me up to eat later!!

4. I am screaming with fear!

5. I have been told to be quiet. That must mean it is bad to show your feelings. STIFF UPPER LIP.

6. SOME YEARS LATER... Nowadays none of us show our feelings. That is good.

7. We love one another but we never say so. That is as it should be.

8. Touching or embracing would be a sign of weakness.

You're six, darling. Time for boarding school.

You'll have a great time! I wish I was your age again!

Bye, honey! Keep smiling! BYE!

I am just relieved to have reached age six without being eaten.

13

SOME MORE COMMON MIXED MESSAGES THAT PARENTS SEND THEIR KIDS...

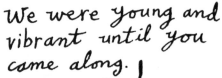

WHY YOU NEED THIS BOOK!

THESE CASE STUDIES SHOW THE VARIOUS FORMS OF EMOTIONAL DAMAGE WHICH IS ROOTED, OF COURSE, IN CHILDHOOD. LOOK FOR YOURS HERE.

i - AN INABILITY TO COMMUNICATE.

How are you?

Fine. ←

THIS SINGLE SMALL WORD SPECTACULARLY FAILS TO TRANSMIT THE USER'S FEELINGS OF: LONELINESS; ISOLATION; LOSS OF PURPOSE; FEAR OF DEATH; BELIEF THAT THE WORLD IS WITHOUT POINT; FUTILITY; HELPLESSNESS; HORROR; AND SO ON...

ii - AN INABILITY TO LOVE YOURSELF.

I'm ugly, aren't I?

I'm stupid, aren't I?

My bottom's too big... isn't it?

iii - AN INABILITY TO BE INTIMATE.

I really like you... May I have a kiss? Have you ever seen a clitoris?

Uh! AAH!!

If I'm intimate I will be sucked up inside the other person and DESTROYED!

iv - AN INABILITY TO BE LESS THAN PERFECT.

I must achieve.

Failure is impossible!

If I fail noone will like me!

V – AN INABILITY TO BE YOURSELF.

I must be what others want me to be.

Vi – AN INABILITY TO BELIEVE IN YOURSELF.

I've made lots of money...

I've got ten degrees...

But I'm a failure as a parent.

vii – AN INABILITY TO ENJOY STRAIGHTFORWARD RELATIONSHIPS.

Spank me! People who punish me are showing that they care about me!

SMACK!

viii – AN INABILITY TO BE WRONG.

It's other people who are always wrong.

No, we're not!

See?

ix – AN INABILITY TO ASK FOR WHAT YOU NEED.

I feel fed up and lonely and I want a cuddle....

– But instead of saying that, I'll be grumpy and confrontational which will push people away so that I can indulge in feeling even MORE fed up and lonely...

X – AN INABILITY TO SEE THAT YOU HAVE A PROBLEM.

I don't have a problem, I have a solution! I dress as a woman to access my feelings!

PART 2
THE THERAPIES

BEFORE
(page one)

AFTER
(page sixty four)

WHAT IS THERAPY?

If _LIFE_ is the crazed knitter who turns your thoughts and feelings into an ill-fitting pair of socks, then _THERAPY_ is the steadfast old lady who spends hours unravelling them again.

SO, LET'S GET STARTED...

HERE ARE A FEW OF THE THINGS YOU WILL NEED:

A COUCH OR COMFY CHAIR.

BLAND ABSTRACT ART.

Aargh! It's a picture of my mother biting the heads off my dolls!

POT PLANTS.

A CLOCK FOR TIMING YOUR SESSIONS.

BOXES OF TISSUES (IT IS OKAY TO CRY).

ALL THE ABOVE ITEMS CAN BE PURCHASED FROM THE MR CONCERNED RETAIL THERAPY OUTLET ON PAGE 60.

HOW TO USE THIS BOOK:

DEAR CLIENT, EVEN A MODERN MARVEL LIKE THIS CANNOT WORK ITS WONDERS WITHOUT YOUR CO-OPERATION. ON THE NEXT PAGE YOU'LL FIND SOME SUGGESTIONS TO HELP YOU ENGAGE SUCCESSFULLY IN THE THERAPEUTIC PROCESS.

i – Keep the book in a quiet room where you are unlikely to be disturbed and consult it regularly.

ii – Work from the beginning to the end and complete each session. Don't cheat! The exercises have been scientifically designed to dismantle your brain, clean it, polish it and reassemble it in time to impress your relations at the next family gathering.

iii – When prompted, talk to the book in a strong, clear voice. Be honest, and don't be shy. Complete confidentiality is assured. Unless you happen to be using the book in a bus, train, café or other public place where someone could overhear.

Then he took out his penis and...

WARNING! STARTING THE BOOK BUT FAILING TO COMPLETE IT COULD BE DANGEROUS!

CLARIFYING YOUR ISSUE(S)

You will get more out of this book if you have a clear agenda, so decide on an issue you want to work through. If you can't think of an issue, or can't choose between hundreds, use the issue selector below. Simply close your eyes and plunk down a finger...

Your Mum & Dad	Feeling lost & directionless	Your Mum & Dad	Feeling lost & directionless
Feeling lost & directionless	Your Mum & Dad	Feeling lost & directionless	Your Mum & Dad
Your Mum & Dad	Feeling lost & directionless	Your Mum & Dad	Feeling lost & directionless
Feeling lost & directionless	Your Mum & Dad	Feeling lost & directionless	Your Mum & Dad
Your Mum & Dad	Feeling lost & directionless	Your Mum & Dad	Feeling lost & directionless
Feeling lost & directionless	Your Mum & Dad	Feeling lost & directionless	Your Mum & Dad

DON'T FORGET TO COMPLETE THE FORM BELOW
AND SIGN IT BEFORE CONTINUING!

CONSENT FORM &
CHANGE CONTRACT

Dear Mr Concerned,

I want to explore and then dump the following baggage:

FOR OFFICIAL
USE ONLY!
ARE YOU
OFFICIAL? NO!
THEN LEAVE
THESE BOXES
ALONE!

1: _____ ☐

2: _____ ☐

3: _____ ☐

And if anything were to go terribly, terribly wrong I absolve Mr Concerned, the publishers & the artist from any blame whatsoever.

DATE: _____   SIGNED: _____

TO ENABLE ME TO EVALUATE THE LONG-TERM
SUCCESS OF THIS TALKING HOME THERAPY COURSE,
PLEASE FILL IN THE SLIP BELOW AND RETURN IT
AFTER FINISHING THE BOOK. OR RIGHT NOW WILL DO.

- ✂

My dear Mr Concerned,

It is now over ☐ years since I completed your very marvellous course. I felt I just HAD to write and say that I still feel wonderful/terrific/fabulous.* I also look better/am richer/enjoy better sex* than I did/was* before reading your book. Thank you, thank you, thank you!   Yours, _____

*DELETE SOME WORDS SO THAT REPLIES VARY FOR USE AS TESTIMONIALS.

21

REALITY GRAPH

AS YOU WORK YOUR WAY THROUGH THE COURSE OF THERAPY OUTLINED IN THIS BOOK, PLOT YOUR PROGRESS BY COUNTING THE DAYS ON THE GRAPH BELOW:

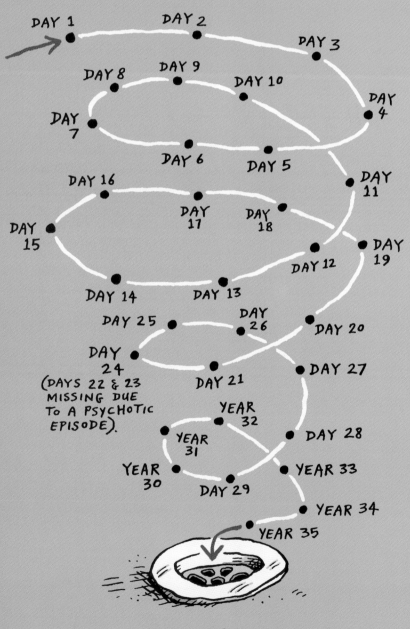

DAY 1
DAY 2
DAY 3
DAY 8
DAY 9
DAY 10
DAY 4
DAY 7
DAY 6
DAY 5
DAY 11
DAY 16
DAY 17
DAY 18
DAY 15
DAY 19
DAY 12
DAY 14
DAY 13
DAY 25
DAY 26
DAY 20
DAY 24
(DAYS 22 & 23 MISSING DUE TO A PSYCHOTIC EPISODE).
DAY 27
DAY 21
YEAR 32
YEAR 31
DAY 28
YEAR 30
YEAR 33
DAY 29
YEAR 34
YEAR 35

22

GETTING STARTED

YOU'LL GAIN THE MOST BENEFIT FROM THIS BOOK IF YOU APPROACH THE EXERCISES WITH A RELAXED AND OPEN FRAME OF MIND. TO THAT END I HAVE SUGGESTED A COUPLE OF STRESS-RELIEVING THERAPY SESSIONS TO BEGIN WITH.

QUICK TIP number 1

SOAKING IN A HOT TUB THERAPY.

Relax in a deep, foamy tub of scalding water and feel your troubles wash away. Visualise them disappearing down the plug hole.

How about doing some role-play work as you soak? Take some plastic figures and a few boats into the bath with you. WARNING! Unlike a real therapist, who could share your bath without damage, this book should NOT be taken into the water. Prop it up on a window ledge or on the dirty-laundry basket.

BACK TO CHILDHOOD THERAPY

IF YOU ARE USED TO WORKING HARD ALL THE TIME RELAXING CAN BE DIFFICULT. TRY THESE EXERCISES BASED ON THE STRESS-FREE DAYS OF CHILDHOOD.

EXERCISE No. 1 ~ SLOUCH IN A CHAIR.

Is this right?

Oh dear, no. Lean back and SLUMP more!

2 ~ TWIDDLE WITH YOUR HAIR.

3 ~ SUCK YOUR THUMB.

SLURP...

4 ~ BREAK TOYS.

CLUNK!

much harder than it sounds.

5 ~ EAT WITH YOUR FINGERS.

Wonderful! No worry about which knife and fork to use!

6 – LIE ON THE FLOOR CHEWING THE CORNER OF A FAVOURITE BLANKET.
Now you're just being silly!
Mng mnng?
GET UP!
Oh dear. Relaxing is SO stressful!

DISCOVERING YOUR INNER CHILD

NOW THAT YOU ARE NICELY RELAXED, I'D LIKE YOU TO TRY AND VISUALISE YOUR CHILD WITHIN...

i – START BY POURING YOURSELF A STIFF DRINK.

Surely my inner child shouldn't be getting drunk?

ii – CLOSE YOUR EYES & BREATHE DEEPLY... IN... OUT... IN...

Poo! My inner child needs a nappy change!

iii – <u>BECOME</u> YOUR INNER CHILD...

Goo!

Suddenly 'goo' makes complete sense.

QUICK TIP number ②

NOSTALGIA THERAPY

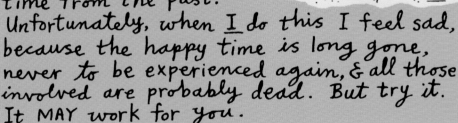

Cheer yourself up by visualising a happy time from the past.
Unfortunately, when <u>I</u> do this I feel sad, because the happy time is long gone, never to be experienced again, & all those involved are probably dead. But try it. It MAY work for you.

REGRESSION THERAPY

CONCENTRATING ON YOUR INNER CHILD,
CAST YOUR MIND BACK TO YOUR VERY
FIRST MEMORY OF BEING A HAPPY BABY...

PRESS BUTTON (A)

1 - Now, gurgle, laugh & be sick on your mum.

PRESS BUTTON (B)

2 - Jump forward in time. It is your first day at school and your mother has just left you. You are crying loudly.

PRESS BUTTON (D)

3 - Time passes again. Now you are an ugly, spotty and rather overweight pubescent teenager. Say nothing... in as sullen and sulky a manner as you can manage.

PRESS BUTTON (C)

4 - More time passes. You are dating. Tell me about your first sexual fumblings.

PRESS BUTTON (E)

5 - We're really starting to make progress, which means it's time to...

PRESS BUTTON (F)

FINDING YOURSELF

SOUNDS EASY, DOESN'T IT? BUT HOW MANY
OF US GO THROUGH THE WHOLE OF OUR
LIVES FEELING LIKE FRAUDS BECAUSE
WE DON'T KNOW WHO WE REALLY ARE?
MOST OF US ARE DEFINED BY HOW OTHERS
SEE US. TRY ASKING YOUR FRIENDS AND
RELATIONS WHO THEY THINK <u>YOU</u> ARE!

SO WHO ARE YOU DEEP DOWN INSIDE? A
MIXTURE OF ALL THE ABOVE, OR SOMEONE
ELSE ENTIRELY...

28

HIDE & SEEK THERAPY

THIS IS A FUN WAY TO FIND YOURSELF USING VISUALISATION.

Imagine you are back in your childhood home. The first floor represents the conscious, ground floor the subconscious, and basement the inherited subconscious.

Pretend that the REAL you is hiding somewhere in the house... but what's that creaking sound? Listen, was that a giggle? And where's the spine-chilling music coming from?

To spice things up a little I've added a race against time. You must find yourself before a psycho, loose in the house, does – or you'll end up strangled, dismembered and packed into an assortment of luggage and hat boxes. Phew! Isn't the imagination a powerful tool?

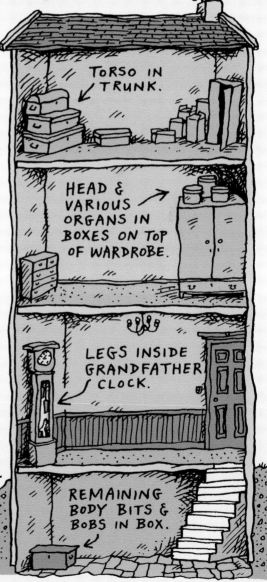

TORSO IN TRUNK.

HEAD & VARIOUS ORGANS IN BOXES ON TOP OF WARDROBE.

LEGS INSIDE GRANDFATHER CLOCK.

REMAINING BODY BITS & BOBS IN BOX.

29

MULTIPLE PERSONALITIES

IF YOU'RE HAVING DIFFICULTY FINDING YOURSELF IT COULD BE BECAUSE THERE ISN'T JUST ONE 'YOU'. THERE ARE MANY!

FOR EXAMPLE, HERE ARE A FEW OF MINE:

A FEW YEARS AGO I HAD A PARTICULARLY DULL AND BORING CLIENT WHO TURNED OUT TO CONTAIN THIRTY-SEVEN PERSONALITIES — ALL EXACTLY THE SAME!

RE-INVENT YOURSELF THERAPY

It's no good just putting on a wig and a different pair of trousers and calling yourself Harold.

fig a ~ OLD, DULL BOB.

fig b ~ NEW, DULL BOB.

Actually, I'm Harold.

You must RE-TRAIN yourself inside so that your beliefs, thoughts and automatic reactions are new, too!

Have fun designing the new you. Decide whether you like tea or coffee. Do you listen to classical music or Bing Crosby? Do you enjoy sex, or put up with it?

Now comes the tricky part. Learn to like the things the new you likes by <u>rewarding</u> yourself for listening to Bing and <u>punishing</u> yourself for putting on a Mozart CD.

You'll be surprised how quickly your tastes change!

OLD BIGOTED SHIRLEY.
I hate cities!

NEW BIGOTED SHIRLEY.
I hate the country!

QUICK TIP number 3

PUT ON A DIFFERENT HAT THERAPY

Similar to BUY ALL THE SHOES IN THE SHOP therapy, & START COLLECTING CARS therapy, only cheaper.

Try on balaclavas, swimming caps, homburgs, woolly hats, etc, as a way of identifying the many YOUS.

LYING ON THE FLOOR SCREAMING THERAPY!

THIS IS A VERY EFFECTIVE WAY TO BREAK DOWN THE DEFENSIVE LAYERS WHICH COCOON US FROM OUR 'TRUE' SELVES AND PREVENT US FROM ENJOYING 'REAL' EXPERIENCES OF THE WORLD.

{ MACHO LAYER IN MEN.
{ GIRLIE LAYER IN WOMEN.

PRETENDING NOT TO BE GOOD AT THINGS (WHILE IN FACT BEING OKAY) IN ORDER TO ELICIT PRAISE.

SAYING HORRID THINGS TO MAKE PEOPLE FEEL BAD, THUS PUSHING THEM AWAY SO THAT THEY'LL BE HORRID BACK SO THAT YOU'LL FEEL JUSTIFIED IN BEING HORRID IN THE FIRST PLACE.

THE NICE PERSON INSIDE.

ANOTHER HORRID PERSON.

PHEW! ANOTHER NICE PERSON!

IT'S IMPOSSIBLE TO LIVE A LIFE TRUE TO YOUR-SELF INSIDE ALL THOSE LAYERS, SO TURN TO THE NEXT PAGE AND LET'S GET RID OF THEM...

QUICK TIP number

It is, of course, very possible that beneath all those layers is nothing at all. In that event, take solace from the fact that 'nothing' can't have any problems.

1 – Lie on your back on the floor.

PRESS BUTTON Ⓐ

2 – Scream loudly and kick your feet.

PRESS BUTTON Ⓑ

3 – Scream again, kick your feet and hammer your fists on the floor.

PRESS BUTTON Ⓒ

4 – Scream and scream and scream, kicking and hitting the floor as hard as you can.

PRESS BUTTON Ⓓ

5 – Scream some more and rock from side to side. Ignore the doorbell.

PRESS BUTTON Ⓔ

6 – Howl, scream, shout, wail and whimper. Continue to ignore the doorbell, the banging on the windows and cries of 'Are you alright in there?'

PRESS BUTTON Ⓕ

7 – Make yourself a nice cup of tea...

BACK TO NATURE THERAPY

IT IS POSSIBLE THAT SOME CLIENTS WILL START TO FEEL 'FLOATY' WHILE USING THIS BOOK. IF THAT HAPPENS TO YOU, DON'T PANIC. IT JUST MEANS THAT YOU HAVE BECOME A LITTLE DETACHED FROM REALITY.

The solution is to 'ground' yourself by imagining putting down roots. Visualise your toes extending and pushing their way down into the earth.

Even better, follow the instructions below.

1 - Buy a giant plant pot and a few bags of compost.*

THIS MAN IS A WALL-FLOWER.

2 - Throw off your clothes and plant yourself thigh-deep.

3 - Try to identify what type of plant you are. Visualise your arms covered in leaves... But what kind? Are they deciduous or ever-green? Do you have

*ALL NECESSARY GARDENING ITEMS ARE ON SALE IN THE MR CONCERNED SHOP, PAGE 60.

thorns and do you bear fruit?
If you're lucky, you'll be an indoor plant able to keep warm and dry and watch TV. If unlucky, you'll be a stick of rhubarb or a Douglas fir out in the garden at the mercy of the elements.

Once you've identified yourself you may want to change. Perhaps you're too pretty or too prickly. Perhaps you smell too strong.

Here are some interesting plants you might like to consider:

a – CACTUS.   b – VENUS' FLY-TRAP.   c – LAWN.
Duck!
Lawnmower
coming!)

Try to spend a couple of hours each week in your pot - but watch out for flirty bees!

QUICK TIP number ⑤

SILENT THERAPY

Say nothing for an entire day. You'll be surprised at how liberating it can be.

If you don't speak to me RIGHT NOW I'm leaving you!

Well?

Come on!

DENIAL THERAPY

THIS IS A USEFUL THERAPY FOR PEOPLE WHO
DON'T WANT TO KNOW WHO THEY REALLY ARE
OR WHAT THEY REALLY FEEL. FOR THEM, DENIAL
CAN BE A VERY SUCCESSFUL WAY OF COPING
WITH LIFE. JUST FOLLOW THIS NON-REALITY-
BASED THERAPEUTIC SURVIVAL REGIME.

STEP 1 ~ EAT CHOCOLATE.

I feel better already!

STEP 2 ~ BELIEVE EVERYTHING PEOPLE TELL YOU.

Do you love me?

Er, um, well, ah, er, yes...

Oh, I KNEW it!

STEP 3 ~ LIVE A COMPULSIVE LIE.

My children love me. My husband loves me. I love myself and I am very happy.

STEP 4 ~ FANTASISE.

A shining knight on a huge white horse is going to take me away from all this and give me a facial.

STEP 5 ~ FIND A FAITH.

God loves me just the way I am. No need to change...

STEP 6 ~ LIVE IN THE FUTURE OR THE PAST BUT NEVER IN THE PRESENT.

Things were great when we first met. And they'll be great again. One day...

36

COLOUR THERAPY

TRY THIS COLOUR MOOD TEST TO
DETERMINE YOUR UNDERLYING STATE OF
MIND AT THIS POINT IN THE BOOK. SIMPLY,
1 – Place your left hand on the page in
the place indicated below.
2 ~ Count to three.   3 ~ Turn over and
consult the colour generator.   4 – Take
appropriate
therapeutic
action!

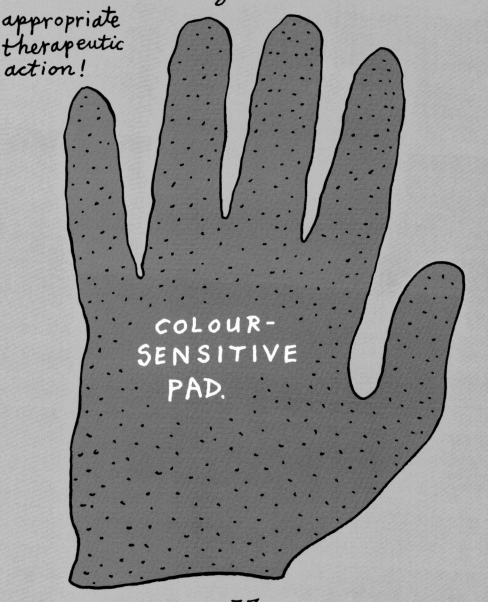

COLOUR-
SENSITIVE
PAD.

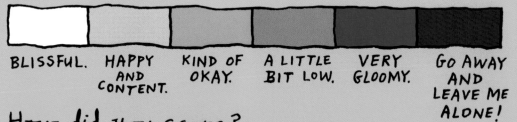

BLISSFUL.   HAPPY   KIND OF   A LITTLE   VERY   GO AWAY
            AND   OKAY.   BIT LOW.   GLOOMY.   AND
            CONTENT.   LEAVE ME
                                                          ALONE!

How did you score?
If 'happy and content' you're doing very
well. Therapy obviously agrees with you.
If, on the other hand, your score is 'Go
away and leave
me alone' then
persevere with
this
book!
Perhaps
even
increase
the
frequency
of your
sessions.

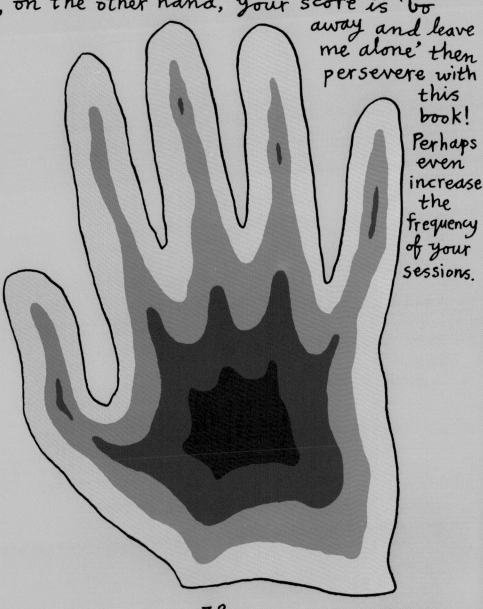

ENDORPHINS ARE USEFUL LITTLE CHEMICALS WHICH THE BODY PRODUCES TO MAKE THE BRAIN FEEL BETTER. HERE ARE SOME WAYS OF GETTING YOUR BODY TO RELEASE THEM:

i - SEX.   ii - LAUGHTER.   iii - EXERCISE.

Don't laugh at me while I'm having sex on my auto-pumper!

Ha ha ha ha ha ha!

Go away and leave me alone!!

You're obviously very gloomy.

QUICK TIP number 6

HAVE A NAP THERAPY

If you find yourself feeling a little 'Go away and leave me alone' you may just be overtired. Try having a nap - and don't forget to jot down any dreams you have. We'll be looking at them on page 55.

a - CATNAP.   b - DOGNAP.   c - HEDGEHOG NAP.

A PERSON NAPPING FOR FIVE MONTHS IN A BOX OF STRAW.   zzzz

RESTRICTIVE THERAPY

HERE'S A SIMPLE, SCIENTIFICALLY PROVEN WAY TO LIFT THE WEIGHT OF DAILY STRESS AND DRUDGERY FROM YOUR SHOULDERS. JUST FOLLOW THESE DIRECTIONS:

1 – BUILD A CAGE USING BASIC WELDING TECHNIQUES.

2 – CLIMB INSIDE & LOCK THE DOOR.

3 – THROW AWAY THE KEY.

4 – SOON...

I can't go to work!

I can't spend money!

I can't do the house-work!

I can't fail to achieve!

5 –

This is amazing! All my dreary daily responsibilities and worries have vanished!

6 –

I'm FREE!

QUICK TIP *number*

EXORCISM THERAPY

Evidence of POLTERGEIST ACTIVITY is a sure sign that you are <u>seriously</u> disturbed. As is reading this book from back to front — the Devil's direction! My advice is to persist with the sessions in this book, but also drink tea made with Holy water. Boil the water, of course. You never know how long it's been stagnating in the font.

SHOULD YOU <u>ACCESS YOUR FEELINGS?</u>

ONE THEORY, WIDELY HELD, IS THAT WE ARE A RACE OF FLESH AND BLOOD ROBOTS BUILT IN A DISTANT, ALIEN LABORATORY AND ABANDONED ON EARTH. AND WHO'S TO SAY IT'S NOT TRUE? PERHAPS, INSTEAD OF TRYING TO GET IN TOUCH WITH OUR

Do you love me?

There is no logical reason to.

FEELINGS, WE SHOULD JUST COME TO TERMS WITH THE FACT THAT WE DON'T HAVE ANY. THEN WE COULD CONCENTRATE ON GUILT-FREE SEX.

41

SAND-BOX ROLE-PLAY THERAPY

A USEFUL AID FOR ACCESSING DEEPLY BURIED FEELINGS. YOU WILL NEED A TRAY, SOME SAND AND THE LITTLE FIGURES OPPOSITE.

1 – Fill the tray with sand.

2 – Place play figures in the tray.

3 – Make the figures interact. Move them about and do their voices. Make them play tennis, have tea and watch TV. Who sleeps with who? Make them fight.

Make them dig graves and murder each other.

A fun therapy for all the family!

Ideal for exploring disturbing dreams...

GET OUT of my sand tray!

↑ FEELING OF ANGER ACCESSED ALREADY!

42

LEARN TO BE POSITIVE

HERE'S AN EXAMPLE OF SIBLING RIVALRY, A COMMON FAMILY ISSUE.

LOOK AT THESE FIVE CUPS CAREFULLY. WHICH IS HALF-FULL AND WHICH HALF-EMPTY?

a-   b-   c-   d-   e-

ANSWER: THEY ARE ALL <u>EXACTLY</u> THE SAME, THANKS TO THE MR CONCERNED™ ATOMIC FLUID DISPENSER!*

*SEE PAGE 60.

My fluid dispenser measures liquids to the individual molecule, thus ensuring absolute fairness! There'll be no sibling rivalry over drinks in the Mr Concerned household!

Dad! Cornwallis drank some of my juice!

Heh heh heh heh...

NEGATIVE THERAPY

IN CONTRAST TO POSITIVE THERAPY, NEGATIVE THERAPY STATES THAT THE WORLD IS POINTLESS, THERE IS NO PURPOSE AND YOU ARE MERELY A MOMENTARY SPECK IN AN INFINITY OF MEANINGLESSNESS.

There now. Doesn't _that_ make your problems shrink into proportion? In the grand scheme of nothing, they are just not worth worrying about.

QUICK TIP number 8

CHAT-SHOW THERAPY

There I am! Don't I look great?!

I'm really a man, Bob!

Boost your confidence by announcing who you are to millions of viewers AND a studio audience! Bask in the knowledge that YOUR problem really is special – and, therefore, YOU are really special, too.

TOUCHY-FEELY THERAPY

Sometimes all that's necessary is a cuddle and a shoulder to cry on. In conventional therapy such physical contact is frowned upon for fear it could awaken sexual feelings between client and therapist. But don't worry. Only a seriously disturbed person could become aroused by a book. Even one as attractive as this.

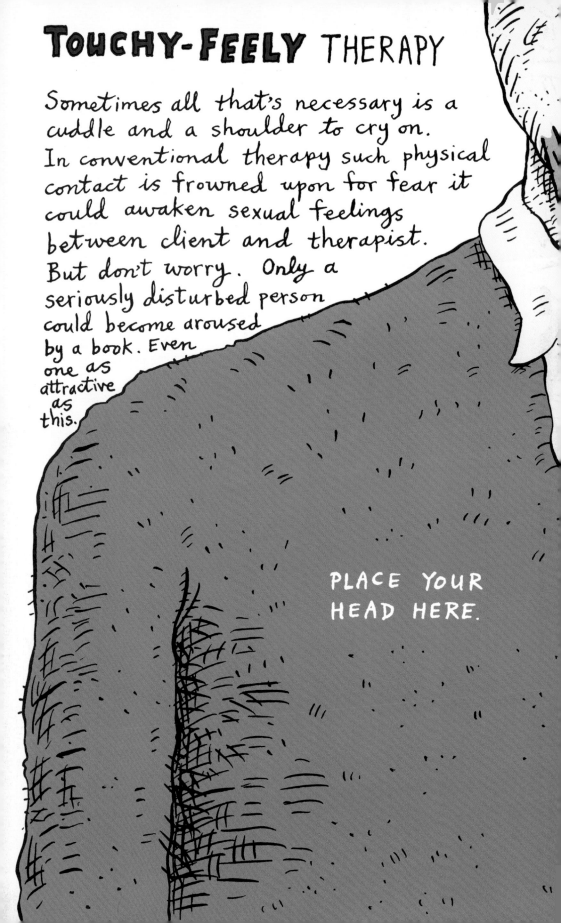

PLACE YOUR HEAD HERE.

INSTRUCTIONS:
Rest your cheek against the artist's impression of my chest. Next, allow your feelings to bubble to the surface. Now, press button Ⓓ. CAUTION! Don't let tears get into the delicate talking mechanism!

sniff... snuffle... sob...

Mr C

Why not order a gorgeously soft Mr Concerned appliquéd v-neck jumper? Makes a great comfort garment. Sale starts Tuesday! See page 60.

THE EMPTY CHAIR

AN IDEAL ROLE-PLAY THERAPY FOR CONCLUDING UNFINISHED BUSINESS WITH AN OGRE FROM YOUR PAST, SUCH AS A PARENT, TEACHER OR SCHOOL BULLY.

1- Invite the person concerned to sit in this drawing of a chair. Visualise them seated.

2- Give them a piece of your mind.

3- Ignore their feeble protestations and press the first two buttons at the bottom of the page.

4- Chuckle to yourself and savour the moment before pressing the remaining buttons.

5- Laugh maniacally!

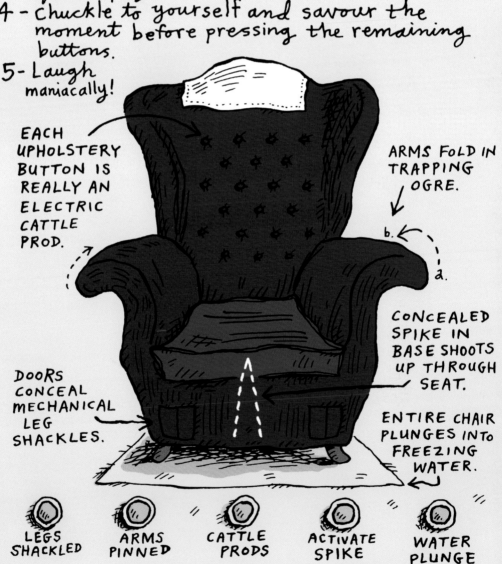

EACH UPHOLSTERY BUTTON IS REALLY AN ELECTRIC CATTLE PROD.

ARMS FOLD IN TRAPPING OGRE.

b.

a.

CONCEALED SPIKE IN BASE SHOOTS UP THROUGH SEAT.

DOORS CONCEAL MECHANICAL LEG SHACKLES.

ENTIRE CHAIR PLUNGES INTO FREEZING WATER.

LEGS SHACKLED — ARMS PINNED — CATTLE PRODS — ACTIVATE SPIKE — WATER PLUNGE

SOME SEXUAL THOUGHTS...

SEX IS, OF COURSE, THE ROOT AND THE ROUTE OF ALL EVIL. IT IS ALSO THE ROOT AND ROUTE OF ALL PLEASURE <u>AND</u> OF PROCREATION. ALL IN ALL, A BIT OF A CONUNDRUM — SO LET'S MOVE RIGHT ALONG & CONSIDER SOME COMMON SEXUAL PROBLEMS.

ONE OF THE MOST COMMON IS GENDER CONFUSION, CLOSELY FOLLOWED BY GUILT. I BET EVEN THE WORD 'GUILT' IS MAKING YOU FEEL GUILTY! WELL, STOP IT... UNLESS FEELING GUILTY ADDS TO YOUR FUN!

Where have my 'bits' gone? Maybe I'm a she...

AN EX-TOM CAT EXPERIENCING GENDER CONFUSION.

QUICK TIP number 9

<u>PRAISE</u> THERAPY

You're wonderful!

Flattery works wonders in a relationship. Here we see Oedipus complimenting his new wife on her cooking:

It's just like my mother's!

INTERMISSION

BY NOW, HALF-WAY THROUGH THIS BOOK, WE ARE GETTING TO KNOW ONE ANOTHER QUITE WELL. WE'VE BEEN LAUGHING TOGETHER AND SHARING INTIMATE SECRETS FOR A WHILE, SO I THINK IT'S TIME YOU PAUSED FOR A MOMENT AND CONSIDERED YOUR MENTAL IMAGE OF ME, YOUR THERAPIST. THE FIRST IMAGE THAT SPRINGS, UNBIDDEN, TO MIND...

IS IT THIS ONE OF THE SERIOUS, DIGNIFIED PROFESSIONAL WORKING TIRELESSLY TO HELP YOU COPE WITH YOUR PROBLEMS?

OR IS IT THIS ONE?

PERHAPS IT'S THIS ONE! STRANGER THINGS HAVE HAPPENED.

BUT OF COURSE! IT'S THIS ONE! NO NEED TO FEEL ASHAMED — EVERYONE ELSE USING THE BOOK WILL HAVE CHOSEN IT TOO!

CHOOSING DRAWING NUMBER FOUR MEANS THAT YOU ARE EXPERIENCING TRANSFERENCE OR, IN LAY TERMS, YOU HAVE

FALLEN IN LOVE WITH YOUR THERAPIST.

This is inevitable, completely natural and should be enjoyed. Let's have no guilty secrets between us!
I love you, too.

COMPUTER-ENHANCED PICTURE.

Of course, many men will be feeling confused and upset at this point. 'Does this mean I am gay?' they'll be asking themselves and their anxious wives. 'Quite probably,' is the answer. But isn't it better to know sooner rather than later?

The other likelihood is that you are bibliosexual. A lesser disruption, since falling in love with a book is far less likely to cause trouble with your partner than falling in love with a flesh and blood therapist. Another plus for this book!

Finally, it's now time for a rather controversial, though fun, sexual therapy...

51

SURROGATE THERAPY

IN THIS THERAPY THE SURROGATE (USUALLY THE THERAPIST) TAKES THE PLACE OF THE CLIENT'S REGULAR SEXUAL PARTNER. THIS MEANS THAT SEXUAL ISSUES CAN BE TACKLED BY THE THERAPIST IN THE BEDROOM, OR IN THE BACK OF A CAR PARKED IN THE WOODS.

Get your regular partner to cut out and wear the mask opposite. He, or she, will be playing the part of ME and must speak ONLY by pressing the buttons on the book.
Ready? Then let the sex therapy begin!

PRESS BUTTON (A)

1 - If I'm not mistaken, that was an invitation to remove your clothes.

PRESS BUTTON (C)

2 - Wasn't that nice! WHAT a positive response to seeing your naked body! Next, I am going to start kissing your knees...

PRESS BUTTON (B)

3 - I think it's time YOU started pleasuring ME... Lower. Across. Up.

PRESS BUTTON (E)

4 - My goodness! We're BOTH about... to...

PRESS BUTTON (D)

5 - Thank you. That was lovely.

PRESS BUTTON (F)

SLEEP-DEPRIVATION THERAPY

Leave me alone!

ASTONISHINGLY, SOME PEOPLE WHO START MY SELF-HELP THERAPY COURSE ACTUALLY SABOTAGE THEIR OWN PROGRESS BY RESISTING THE BOOK!

Mr Appleby, the artist who did the illustrations, was like that. Whenever he was fed up and therefore needed a therapy session the most, he didn't feel like doing it! Well, I soon sorted HIM out, thanks to SLEEP DEPRIVATION — a tried and tested therapeutic technique for breaking down resistant clients. Here's what you do:

1 - Press button Ⓑ and hold it down. Balancing a pile of heavy books on a pencil should do the trick.

2 - The repetition of my voice will keep you awake until you are ready to tell me all your sordid secrets — just like Mr Appleby!

AND HOW DOES THAT MAKE YOU FEEL?

NORMAL SEX

The annotated CAPTAIN STAR

PENCIL.

BOOKS LEANING AGAINST WALL.

54

DREAM INTERPRETATION THERAPY

IF YOU MANAGE TO FALL ASLEEP YOU WILL PROBABLY DREAM, AND DREAMS, OF COURSE, ARE VERY USEFUL WINDOWS INTO THE SUBCONSCIOUS!

Understanding your dreams can make a big contribution to understanding your problems. Here's an example:

I'm dreaming of a white Christmas...

Ah, now the snow obviously represents a frozen emotional landscape, beneath which your feelings, blackened by frostbite, lie buried and inaccessible!

Easy-peasy. But not all dreams are this straightforward. The wily sub-conscious, to protect its nefarious activities, scrambles dreams in order to disguise their meaning. Dreaming of sweets (a sweet dream), for example, is a desire for death from overeating and excess. Here's a final observation:

QUESTION:

ANSWER:

A COMMON RECURRING MALE DREAM IS TO BE CHASED, NAKED, BY A GIANT PENIS-EATING FROG.

WHAT DOES THIS MEAN?

YOU'LL HAVE TO BUY MY BOOK 'AN A-Z OF PENIS-EATING DREAMS' (COMPANION VOLUME TO 'LADIES' POLITE DREAMS') BECAUSE WE'VE RUN OUT OF SPACE!

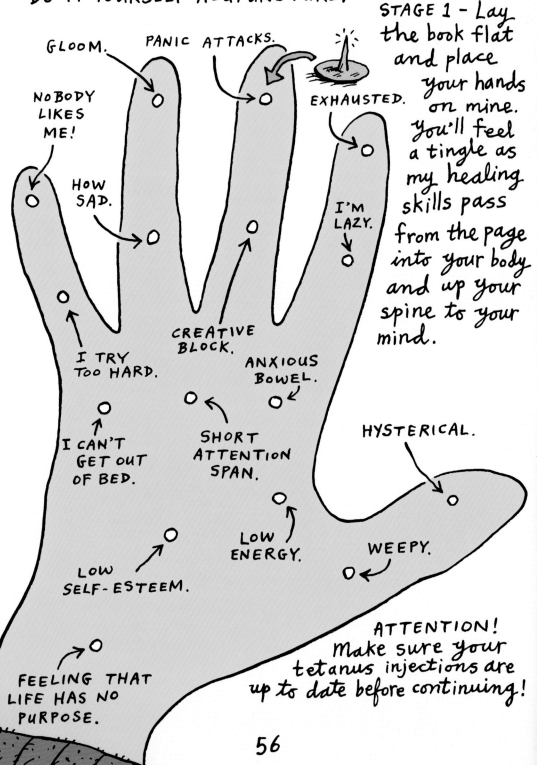

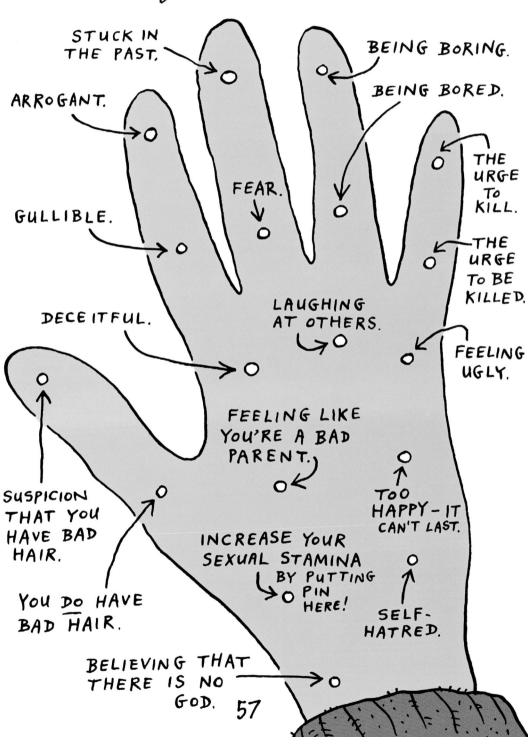

POSITIVE AFFIRMATION THERAPY

LET'S START BY PRESSING BUTTON Ⓒ

THERE'S NOTHING QUITE AS UPLIFTING AS HEARING SOMETHING POSITIVE ABOUT YOURSELF.

The handy, pocket-sized device below is designed to FLOOD you with powerful, confidence-building UNCONDITIONAL POSITIVE REGARD...

INSTRUCTIONS:

1- CUT OUT (OR PHOTOCOPY & CUT OUT) THE SQUARE OPPOSITE. CREASE THE DIAGONAL LINES & THE PARALLEL LINES:

2- OPEN OUT & PLACE FACE DOWN ON THE TABLE. FOLD THE FOUR CORNERS INTO THE CENTRE:

i -   ii -

3- TURN OVER & FOLD THE FOUR CORNERS INTO THE CENTRE AGAIN:

i -   ii -   iii - FOLD IN HALF:

4- SLIP THUMB & FIRST FINGER OF BOTH HANDS BENEATH NUMBER SQUARES:

5- OPERATE AS SHOWN BY ARROWS

i - PICK A NUMBER (eg. 4).
ii - COUNT ALOUD (1, 2, 3, 4,) AS YOU OPEN & CLOSE DEVICE 4 TIMES. iii - NOW CHOOSE A COLOUR (e.g. RED). iv - SPELL R, E, D, AS YOU OPEN & CLOSE DEVICE. v - CHOOSE COLOUR AGAIN. vi - READ MANTRA.

SOME MORE UNCONDITIONALLY POSITIVE PHRASES FOR YOU TO WALLOW IN:

i - You are gorgeous!   ii - You are cool.

iii - You are handsome.   iv - You are infallible.

v - You are marvellous.   vi - You are the best!

vii - You are astonishing.   viii - You should rule the world!

ix - Honestly! I mean it! In fact, you should rule the universe...

OF COURSE, PLEASE DISREGARD <u>ALL</u> THE ABOVE POSITIVE STATEMENTS IF THEY DO <u>NOT</u> APPLY TO YOU!

HELLO, DEAR CLIENT, WE ARE ALONE AGAIN,
SO LET'S INDULGE IN SOME FRANTIC, UPLIFTING

RETAIL THERAPY!

You'll soon be floating on air as you spend,
spend, spend on the delicious Mr Concerned™
items, below (to ground yourself again return to p.34).

The **BUMPER BARGAIN**
THERAPY STARTER
PACK!
INCLUDES:
COUCH,
PLANTS,
PICTURES,
CLOCK &
2 DOZEN
BOXES OF
EMOTIONALLY
ABSORBENT
TISSUES!

FREE! WITH EVERY
ORDER OVER
A SECRET, SURPRISE
AMOUNT... A **BOX**
OF TISSUES PRINTED
WITH Mr Concerned's
FACE!

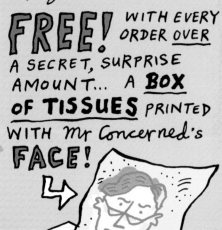

Mr Concerned's
HIGHLY ABSORBENT
TISSUES!
MOP UP YOUR LIFE!

THE Mr Concerned **POSITIVE**
AFFIRMATION BEAN-BAG
DOLL!

PRESS

You are a
valuable
Person!

KEEP HIM IN
YOUR POCKET OR
HANDBAG AND
PRESS HIS TUMMY
WHEN YOU FEEL LOW.

WHY NOT VISIT THE *air-conditioned* Mr Concerned™ INTERNET SHOP

WHERE OUR FRIENDLY STAFF ARE WAITING TO SERVE YOU COMPLIMENTARY CUPS OF TEA OR COFFEE AS YOU BROWSE.

CHILD-PROOF LID!

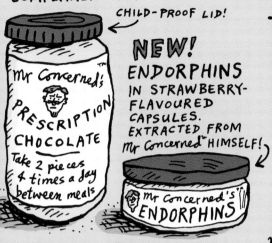

Mr Concerned's™
PRESCRIPTION
CHOCOLATE
Take 2 pieces
4 times a day
between meals

NEW! ENDORPHINS IN STRAWBERRY-FLAVOURED CAPSULES. EXTRACTED FROM Mr Concerned™ HIMSELF!

Mr Concerned's ENDORPHINS

The SMART SARCOPHAGUS!

THEY SAY THAT LIFE IS ALL ABOUT HAVING EXPERIENCES, RIGHT? **WRONG!** IN FACT, THE ONLY WAY TO GET THROUGH LIFE PSYCHOLOGICALLY UNSCATHED IS TO <u>PROTECT</u> YOURSELF FROM EXPERIENCE INSIDE THE Mr Concerned™ SMART SARCOPHAGUS!

THE Mr Concerned INFLATABLE SEXUAL SURROGATE!

7 WORKING ORIFICES!

IMPORTED. made of best quality VULCANISED RUBBER! INCLUDES SPARE PENIS!

ALL FOOD IS TRANSFORMED TO TASTE LIKE STRAWBERRIES.

'I hate you' IS TRANSLATED BY THE HEARING FILTER INTO 'I love you.'

ALL THINGS SEEN ARE MADE TO APPEAR ATTRACTIVE.

COOL DECAL!

The GROUND YOURSELF GARDENING SET.

HUMAN

HUMAN COMPOST
HYGENIK NUTRITIONN

GIANT POT. →

David

FREE NAME STAKE.

THICK SKIN IS TOTALLY EMOTION-PROOF.

NO FEET SO NO RISK OF STANDING IN ANY-THING YUKKY.

INCLUDES BUILT-IN NO MAINTENANCE CHEMICAL TOILET.

ARE <u>YOU</u> A
WINNER OR A LOSER?

IN THIS FINAL THERAPY SESSION YOU
ARE GOING TO LET <u>FATE</u> LEND A HAND,
JUST AS SHE DOES IN LIFE, AND USE
A DICE TO HELP YOU ACHIEVE CLOSURE AND
THUS CLOSE THE BOOK FOR THE LAST
TIME. UNTIL YOU NEED IT AGAIN.

STEP 1 - *Choose one of the three dice below:*

WINNERS'
DICE:

LOSERS'
DICE:

NORMAL
DICE:

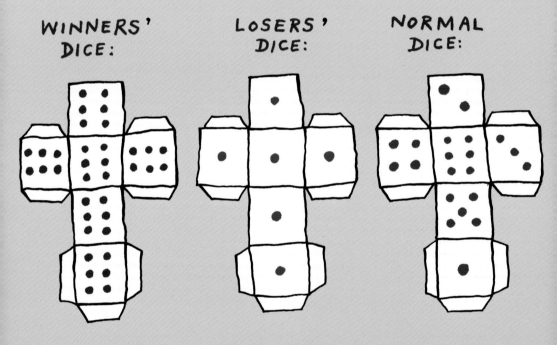

STEP 2 - *Cut out and assemble your
dice.*
FINALLY - *Close your eyes, shake the
dice and throw it...*

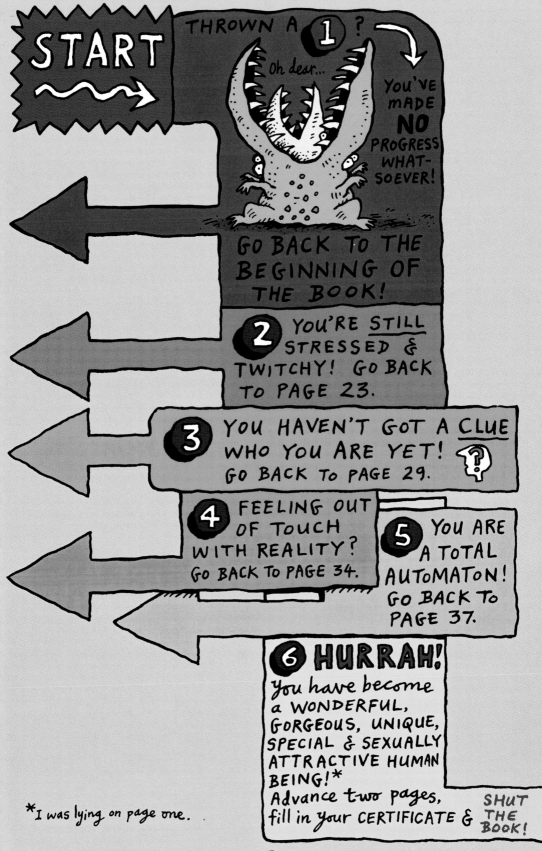

MANAGING AN UNEXPECTEDLY ABRUPT TERMINATION OF THERAPY

Just imagine, for a moment, the awful scene should your book suddenly fall silent.

ARRGH!! The BATTERY has RUN DOWN!

Naturally, you will be angry with the book. It has rejected you. Don't feel guilty about this. Soon your anger will turn into self-pity. The book doesn't like you. Next will come terror. You are all alone! But DON'T PANIC. Take control of yourself – the situation is easily remedied. Simply go to your bookseller and buy another copy. Or six. Of course, I am thinking ONLY of you! Losing your therapeutic support very suddenly COULD be dangerous. Maybe you should buy ten copies...

IMPORTANT!

DO NOT PLUG THIS BOOK INTO A MAINS ELECTRICITY SUPPLY! A FIRE COULD RESULT!

Mr Concerned's TALKING HOME THERAPY COURSE HAS BEEN SUCCESSFULLY COMPLETED BY:

---- ---- ---- ---- ---- ----

WHO IS NOW A CONTENT, WELL-ADJUSTED, SPECIAL AND IN EVERY WAY WONDERFUL HUMAN BEING. IN FACT, I WOULD HAVE NO HESITATION IN EMPLOYING, MARRYING OR INVITING:

---- ---- ---- ---- ---- ----

TO ONE OF MY HOUSES AS A WEEKEND GUEST — AND THAT'S HIGH PRAISE INDEED!

KEEP THIS CERTIFICATE IN A SAFE PLACE, IT IS ALSO YOUR 3 MONTH WARRANTY VALID FROM THE DATE OPPOSITE.

SIGNED

Segue 'Jim' Concerned.

DATE

(FILL IN DATE HERE)